CHOICES
Poetry for a Positive Direction

By

Reginald O. Johns

To Clyde,
My UVa Brother!
Much success in your
future. May God bless
you & your family.
Reginald Johns
'03

Cover Photo by NA' DERE

ISBN: 0-75962-325-2

This book is printed on acid free paper

1stBooks - rev. 04/07/01

SPEAKING OUT
ABOUT

CHOICES
Poetry for a Positive Direction

I thoroughly enjoyed the experience.
I laughed. I smirked. I contemplated.
I pondered. I smiled. I grew....

I feel honored that you would allow me to read
your thoughts, feelings, fears, concerns....
You poured out!

For all those who will one day be blessed to read this work, "Thank-you!"

There is praise, pain, worship, joy, hope, help,
LIFE
in these pages.

I felt like I was reading my own reality.
I feel inspired.

Again, thank-you.

Your sister in Christ,

Shelly

ACKNOWLEDGMENTS...

To the leadership of Rock Church International, Bishop John Gimenez and Pastor Anne Gimenez, I say thank you for your time, effort, and heart for the Bride of the Lord Jesus Christ. May this literary work testify that your labor is not in vain.

I would like to give God praise for the glorious gifts He bestows to His Church: the prophets - Linda Morris and Arthur King. He used you to bring my gifts to my attention for my cultivation. May God fulfill all of your dreams as you wait upon the Lord.

I also affectionately extend gratitude to my parents, Harold and Marion Johns. You sat me upon your knee and read to me. For this, I am eternally grateful. Those times of sharing made me feel warm, wanted, and loved. What more could a child ask for?

To the Lord Jesus Christ, I give praise for every good thing in this creation.

DEDICATION...

This book is dedicated to the loving memory of Ms. Judith Braithwaite. Following the attendance of your funeral, I was inspired to begin writing after several years of rest. Your homegoing motivated me to follow your example of investing one's life as a seed for Jesus. May your return from your earthly deposit in the children of Hampton Roads prosper you eternally in heaven.

CONTENTS...

Step IV - Purpose

Step V - Progeny

Step VI - Peace

PRAYER

CHOICES

I

    want

       to know

          the wonders

God

Will

   show

    me

      when

       I

         listen

           to

            his

              voice

And

   His

     communion

       becomes

        the

          first

            choice

              of

               my

                 attention.

Reginald O. Johns

REPENTANCE

I still have
a chance
to learn
to try
and succeed

I still have
a chance
to repent
renew
and receive
the life
God
has for
me

FAITH

A word must
receive action
so it is not a waste

Faith takes work
for blessings
to awake

and start running down
that same path
you made through

your faith walk with God
to eventually
overtake you

Reginald O. Johns

BLUEPRINTS

Nothing
new
can ever be
created

if we keep our
eyes on the old
leaving our imaginations
abated

giving us
only
the option
to receive

the
images
others
want us to
believe

Turn off
the TV

Stop listening
to advice

Put your
brain in action

It doesn't work
better on ice

There's no
crime in being
alone

Develop
visions
and plans of
your own

You'll be
surprised
that the blueprint
for your success
is already in your
home

Reginald O. Johns

DAWN

Today
only comes once
don't sleep
and let it pass you by

The fulfillment
of dreams
only needs you
to try

What you need
is in your grasp

It's obtainable
for you

When you
act on the desire

that inwardly motivates you

Silly is in the eye of the beholder
Don't wait! You're getting older

Your expiration date is approaching
Act in faith
Stop looking for coaching

Develop your plan
Who cares if you fail?

You'll never know
what will work

Until **perseverance**
Prevails

WORKS

Now take the chance
to help God's kingdom advance

Wait not for the perfect time
for everything to fall in line

Mix works with your faith
Don't think you have to wait

to begin doing the dream
that's bursting the seams

of your heart where it was birthed
to fulfill God's purpose
for the men of the Earth

Reginald O. Johns

BLESSINGS

Faith takes work
to get it to start

upon the work
of your hands

a blessing
I will impart

designed especially
for you

READ THE CLAUSES

If
is a conditional
word
that keeps me
hanging

on

to find out
what I must
do

the deed
I must
accomplish

to make my
dreams
come true

What power
you hold

my two
letter friend

appearing
in contracts
between nations
again and again

For when
Ifs
are broken
peace
is no
more

But when they
are kept
provision
overflows

God
help me keep
your word
and fulfill every
prophetic promise
my spirit has
heard

GLORY

Who opened
the window?
Who caused the
wind to blow?
Who uncovered
my darkness so
I could know.....

the truth

Who turned
on the light?
Who brought me
to this place?
Where my sin
repulses me
in the light of Your
holy face?

Who opened
my eyes?
Who let me
weigh the real worth
of the pleasures of sin
and the gift of the new birth?

Someone
must have been
praying
with tongues or
understanding
to free me from the pit
that somehow
I was snared in

Reginald O. Johns

Thank you
my great intercessor
Jesus the Christ
for helping me see
clearer
in the glory of
your light

DETHRONED

Friday
I take your
crown

You have
no right
to make
the rest
of the week
feel

Down

Friday
I take your
crown

and
spread
your
jewels
all around

the
rest
of the
work week

giving it
expectancy
that something
great is
awaiting
me

Reginald O. Johns

I
Thank God
for
Monday
and Tuesday
too

even the
Wednesday
when everything
seems
due

Friday
you are
dethroned
brought down
by humility

for
everyday
is God's

Present

to

me

to unwrap
with
surprise
of new adventures
within
every hour
spent

in
living
for God
100 %

STRENGTH TRAINING

Muscles only grow
when we
give them
rest

after
workouts
of tension
and stress

So into your
presence
I come

to rest

with
the wisdom

You used
to make
the world

When I wait on
you
I renew my strength

Your guidance
helps me
makes sense of

the world

Reginald O. Johns

You

put

me

in

STAND

Who can see
the man
that I will
be

when I
become all

God said I
would be

Will they be
surprised

when they
realize

a mighty man
has metamorphosized

before their very
eyes

Don't be amazed when
my fear passes away

and all you can
see is a man of faith

And I become all God
has said to me

and
I choose to stand in His
mighty victory

Reginald O. Johns

UNVEILED

Sometimes
it's
uncomfortable

being watched

like a bodybuilder
on the beach

I guess
I am just a
wonder

of

God's

originality

Now I realize

that from me
others draw

strength

Understanding of God
from His

imprint

To hide God's beauty
would be a crime

For unveiling
it is now time

I destroy this veil
so others can see

God's manifestation
of His glory

Reginald O. Johns

ARCHEOLOGICAL DISCOVERIES

I have found you again!

Where have you been?

Why are you covered
with all this dust,
grime and sin?

How could I have
ever stopped using you?

Why did I listen
to the criticism and abuse?

You were a blessing for me
to uncover and discover

A way for God to use me
unlike any other

You made me different from all the rest
How could I have ever left you alone
Thinking uniformity was best

Time away
is time wasted
I now
know

Cause only
when you
use a gift
will a gift
ever grow

CAUTION: WATCH OUT FOR FALLING BLESSING!

If......
If.....
If.....
If.....

Watch
out
cause
there's more
than
one key

to open the door of
blessing
you've been expecting

You do
your job
Obey what God
says

Let Him
do His thing
cause you never
know what way

His provision
is coming
to
      start
         running
            You over!

Reginald O. Johns

THOUGHTS

If you think that you can't
You're right

If you think you won't
You're right

If you think God can
You're right

If you think God will
You're right

Therefore

Think you can

Think you will

because

God can
and
God will
for you
and
through you
if
you
think
He
can

DECISIONS...DECISIONS...DECISIONS

If bodybuilding was
easy
everyone would
be in
shape

If preparing a meal was
easy
like Martha Stewart
we would
bake

But it's
not as
we know

unless we choose
to grow and learn

of a better way

Though there shall
always be a
rising of the sun
it's not mandatory
how things should
be done

so if you
don't like
your life
learn

of a
better
way

Reginald O. Johns

Though
it may turn out
different from the rest
You'll love the
results
for things turn out best

when we follow
God's way

Jesus Christ

THE RELEASE

I will let you
grow
and release
you from
the hold
I have placed
on you
restraining God's glory
you are well
overdue

I let you
go
and
release you
so everyone
will see
the beauty
and strength
God has created and
purposed for me

Like a body
we all advance
when one is found
strong
Be bold
take a chance
In the winner's circle
you belong

No longer hearken
to the cries of the insane
who want everything
I mean everything

to always

stay the same

Reginald O. Johns

CAN WE TALK?

I sat to myself
content with my memories
of friendships of old
for new ones
I felt no need

Even though my friends were so far away
and their faces I didn't see
regularly every day

My heart closed
and didn't extend
to connect with open hearts

I needed no new friends

Until I feel the need
I'll sit here all alone
Content from the past
share my heart by the phone

Like meat from the freezer
I will draw
laughter, acceptance, and belonging
anecdotes enough to gnaw

But then...

God turned the page
and somehow the experiences
of the past seemed to be erased

No longer did I feel full
from the things that I had done
there was a new hunger for life
a new beginning had begun

Like a space traveler on a mission
I had been dropped
in a brand new place
Learning a new language
needing to know a new face

Depending on others
to supply a basic need
of sharing my life with another
and giving myself as a seed

Taking time to care
to talk and to share
beyond a God bless you
and a smile here and there

Like all married folk know
relationships take time
spent together
in communion
beyond a shallow line

But an imparting
and receiving
need to take place
when two are in each other's presence
beholding face to face

a life that God has created
with beauty, uniqueness, and flaws
without the fear of rejection
because one is made to awe

at a sin that is revealed
from a wound not yet healed
that needs a loving touch
from a friend who would conceal

Reginald O. Johns

a matter for a season
by love which is the reason
he is there as an
agent in action
extending God's
mercy and compassion

LEARNER'S PERMIT

If
If you don't try
you will die
wondering
why
you never
tasted
true
life

If you don't try
you will not
be content
but only
wonder
where
all the time
went

If you sit and wait
without trying your
wings
you will never
fly nor will
you sing
for you will
just die
and continue to
wonder why
you have never tasted
true life

If
you get up...walk a bit and strut... Believe with boldness I can... do something for
this man... you will see.. my glory.... manifested before the sons of men....
through thee.... so the choice... is easy.... repent... and turn yourself on...and you
will learn....it's much more fun.... to be behind the wheel... than to sit in driver's
education class... taking notes...and...sitting still

PURPOSE

Truth
spoken
makes
chains
broken

Love
given
makes
life worth
living

Longsuffering
used
heals the
abused

Forgiveness
extended
makes
wounded hearts
mended

Whatever your
ailment
stay not
in derailment

In you
is the key
to set
another
free

Church has
a purpose
beyond offering
collection

Through the
utilization of
the saints
we all mature
to perfection

Reginald O. Johns

THE BREAD OF LIFE

Bake it
in the oven

Break it,
we'll be
loving

the bread of life
in you

Give
you'll be
receiving

a blessing
beyond
believing

the bread of life
in you

Grinded
and pounded
kneaded
and stretched

God's workings
in our lives
we should never forget

is to be
bread
for many

an example
of Christ
for those
without any

training
from a
grandmother's knee
or Sunday school
lessons from
a nursery

Like manna
God gave to help
the Israelites survive

Sometimes we
are dropped
in places to
our surprise

where we
are given by
our faithful Father
who provides

the Bread of life

Reginald O. Johns

WELL WORTH THE WAIT

Who can sleep
when the river's flowing
Who can stay still
When God is showing
Himself to man
again and again

The angels cry Holy
because they see no sin
only the glory
of His presence

What a sight to see
So don't you see now
why I am not sleepy

only desiring to take a look at Your face
Jesus will be my rock
You can't kill me in your embrace

Release that drop
of understanding that I need

to fall prostate and like the angels and
cry Holy, Holy, Holy

PRAISE

Reginald O. Johns

THE HOLY SPIRIT

I saw the curtain wave
in the warm wind
and
I knew you had
come in

I felt a glow
on my face
and
the sweetness of
your embrace
and
I knew you had
come in

I faced truth
with my eyes
and let go
of my disguise
and
I knew you had
come in

to
set me free
into
sweet
liberty

Thank you God
for coming in

Causing
my life
to begin
again

Reginald O. Johns

DISCOVERIES

I can see
there's a change
I have confidence
in your name

I know you
will
come
whenever
I call

I can see
there's a change
I have confidence
in your name

I know yesterday,
today,
forever,
you are
the same

Where came
this faith?

When in the past
I was so weak?

How do you
strengthen me

as I lay
at your feet?

Like walking in a mist
somehow all of me gets wet

I understand my purpose
I hope I will never forget

That praise opened
this door
that I
had been waiting for

of communion and rest
Victory
and God's best

Reginald O. Johns

SELAH

If today
begins
with a sunrise
will
you rise

with thanksgiving

Or with rain
for the land
will you adore me   ·
with the
lifting of

your hands

What if
I made you
a blanket of
white

causing everything
to sparkle
within your
sight

Would you
sing and dance
with all your
might

In praise
for the days
you are able to enjoy
my child I implore

you to sing today
for tomorrow's
not yours
but mine to give

as well as
abundant life
for those who
in thanksgiving
live

Reginald O. Johns

BLOSSOM

There are some things
that cannot be
explained by
words

No matter
what resources
I have
at hand

Words

can't
express what I
feel in your
presence

like a rose
blossoming
petal by
petal

In your
presence
I become
full

and
opened
to
be
me

and

free

NO RERUNS

If everyday
was
like
today
I would
never grow

If everyday
was like
today
I would
never know

what else
you can
do

how
else
you can
use

me

Therefore,
I thank you
that
every
day

is

Reginald O. Johns

a
different
day
with
new expositions
of your
grace
and mercy

BLUE AND GREEN

Like Blue and Green
You sweep into my
mind
bringing new life
cleansing in time

for the day
that's new
with a vision that's
clear

to become prepared
for Your coming
that's near

I take time
to wait
for you

I take time
to wait
for you

to receive
your instructions
and be endued with
power

renewing my
relationship
with revelation
for this hour

Reginald O. Johns

INTERCESSION

Hummmmm
moan
let it out
until you've grown

or

been delivered
by the anointing
from God's throne

PROPHECY

Reginald O. Johns

NO ASPHALT NEEDED

Don't look
for others to show you
the way

Use your feet to
trod the
way

Tread down
high grasses
and make
a path

Be not
dismayed by
unbelieving believers
who snicker and laugh

What I have
for you
will move you
beyond a position
of rest

A fulfillment
of dreams
that makes
Christ manifest

Reginald O. Johns

STAINED GLASS WINDOWS

What holds back
your light
is it dust
or grime
because you
don't take
the time
to use
my word
and wipe
things that cover
my image in thee
that I want
to shine through
abundantly

Why don't you
take a rag
wash it
through and through
so
others can see
what I'm doing in you

I'm the light
that remains
I do not go out
though I may seem
dim when covered by clout
you give to other things
you consider
more important than me
your source of strength
life and beauty

It's never too late
to give your heart that cleaning
you don't have
to wait till Spring
to act on the meaning

of this poem
that's written
especially for you
my colored glass
that I desire to
shine and live
through

Reginald O. Johns

X-RAY VISION

By His word
He healed
me

By His word
He provided
for me

all
the
things
He
saw
in
me

from
the
beginning

to

the
end

of
the

Christ

in

me

.

When
I
believed
the
report
He
gave
to
me

Reginald O. Johns

A PRAISE OPPORTUNIST

How can I
rejoice
while others
mourn?

How can I
say
thank you Jesus
while others
look forlorn?

But they
kept stirring it
the praise in me

and that Hosanna
the choir
did sing

Could I let
them praise my
God alone?

I had to join in to
exalt the Lord
who is on the throne

So I went to the back
and began to clap my hands

walk in a circle
and praise him in the dance

for no matter
the events of the day

Jesus is worthy
to be praised

MY MEDICINE

Laughter that's
hearty
cleanses me

of the stress
and tension
that try
to bind
me

Off fly
chains
and
I am
set
free

to walk
with Jesus
in His
liberty

Rivers
of living
water
flow
from down deep

lifting me into
the heavens
for a new perspective
to see

of glory and grace
that's been here
all along

and
accessible through
rejoicing in
the God of my
salvation

FROM GLORY TO GLORY

You surround me
You cover me
and you
begin
to love me

just as

I am

Without a word
you reveal to me
a sinful way that
steals from me
my glory
as a man

then

You surround me
You cover me
and you
continue
to love me

just as I am

In your presence
I become intoxicated
making obstacles
become abated
enabling me
to stand

as a man

You surround me
You cover me
and you
continue
to love me

just as I am

You reveal to me
the glory of your plans
and the power
of your hands
and give me
courage to take the land
as your man
when
you surround me
and
cover me
and I allow you
to love me

just

as

I
am

PETER'S LEGACY

Eyes cannot
stop
liberty

Society
cannot
silence

one born
to
be free

Try your
wings
while you
have courage

to soar
above
unbelief

I will hear
and
applaud

stand
at your side
as you show
them all

that miracles
are for today
and God, our Father,
still answers
prayer

Reginald O. Johns

for even if you're
sinking in the ocean
I am still
there

Pleased by
your boldness
and acts of faith

to walk on water
while others
watch and wait

Nth POWER

Don't ever think
the well
has run
dry

There's enough for all
if you will get up
and
try

Ask
the Father
to bless it

He gets
great results

Remember
the widow
with the oil

who had only
enough for her son
and herself

Remember the
boy who
only had
a lunch

Jesus blessed it
and it fed
a real big bunch

Think what you
have is too small

Reginald O. Johns

Go to
praising
and magnify

the great multiplier
who reigns
on High

THE GOD FACTOR

Factor in God
and see
there's nothing impossible

Factor in God
and see
there's nothing insurmountable

He has power
to be tapped

and rivers
to be sapped

Fountains
to be washed in

Forgiveness
for all sin

Plans
to be embraced

and the holiness
of His face

That shall change
and rearrange

you by the power
of His grace

Reginald O. Johns

TIME

Sunrise
waits not
for one
who sleeps
too late

Sunset
has a habit
not to stop
nor delay

for one who finds
other things to do

than fulfilling the purpose
of the life given to you

Our days
are numbered

The hour glass
has been turned

Time
like money
is too valuable
to be burned

DREAMS

Don't give up
on your
hopes and dreams

Things are not
as bleak as
they seem

For there is
one working behind
the scenes

making sure that
all things
work together
for the good
for thee

Reginald O. Johns

PURPOSE

If I told you
everything
would you believe

the mighty
plan
I have for thee

I tell you
in part
by a prophet or a dream

so you would
search out
my word
to find stones in a stream

to sling at
Goliaths
that try to
psyche you out

with their words
of unbelief
profanity and
doubt

Behind my word
I'll put my power
to slay your
Goliaths
this very hour

Get ready
and practice
with your stones

Your strength comes
from me
your God
alone

Sing psalms
to me
rejoice and sing

And I will
continue to
unveil my
Son in thee

Reginald O. Johns

THE LIVING WORD

Sing
Dance
Rejoice in God's presence

Celebrate
Bow
lay prostrate
in reverence

Bring Him
near with
a thank you
or two

Allow His
Holy Spirit
to liberate you

wash
and make new
the man
you see

by His living
Word
the incorruptible
seed

UP, UP, AND AWAY

Bing Bing Bing
Boing Boing Boing

Bounced
the Blue Ball

to the Moon
it was going

At least I wanted it to
with my small little hands

as I forced it to the ground
and watched to find where it would land

How can something ever
get out of this atmosphere

with gravity bringing
things down everywhere

then....

out of nowhere came a jet
soaring over my head

reminding me of a rocket
painted fire engine red

only needing to be pointed
in the right direction

to split the sky in two
without confetti or confection

from parades and onlookers
screaming a heart felt cheer

Reginald O. Johns

A rocket's fuel unaffected by praise
doubts of others, intimidating fear

only needing an internal flame
to combust and ignite

like potential energy awaits
you to help you take flight

Break barriers with your strength
eternal and divine

stirred up and activated
by taking the time

to wave the flame and
make the connection

with the Lord of your creation
who will map out your direction

through the stars
up to the heavens

bringing strength from the inside
beneath your frame

empowering you to soar
and bring glory to His name

MOVE OVER

if a bird can fly
why shouldn't I

enjoy the
sky

move over

if a bird can fly
why shouldn't I

glide over
a cloud

above the
smog

move over

if a bird can fly
why shouldn't I

there's enough room
up in his envi

if a bird can sing
why shouldn't I

chirp an offering

move over

Be it by airplane
or accompaniment track

Reginald O. Johns

I'll find a way to fly
God's got my back

So if you're a bird

get out of my way
because in that blue sky you're enjoying
I'm taking my place

.

DEVELOP YOUR GIFT

Polish and
shine
take your
time
and
develop your
gift

It will
make
room
for you

and will
prosper you
too

Develop
your gift
be it
singing, dancing,
or administration

developed gifts in men
produce
standing ovations

When jobs
are
well done

Promotions
will
come

and you can
give glory
to the God of
your salvation

Reginald O. Johns

OFFERING TIME

Can you say
"Hallelujah!"
or
sing a song of
praise?

Can you
lift your
hands
with your arms
upraised?

Can you
turn around
or
dance
to the beat?

Clap
your hands
or shuffle
your shod feet?

I have
supplied your
every need
according to My
riches in glory.

So
into My
presence
do not come
empty

come with your
firstfruits
of
praise
and
thanksgiving.

Reginald O. Johns

REPENT, THE KINGDOM OF GOD IS AT HAND

When tomorrow comes
will you be satisfied
just knowing the will of God
and never having tried

to step out on water
lay your hands on the sick
cast out devils
speak with tongues
or be obedient to give

Oh, if I had what
brother so and so got
I would do this and that

You better be
thankful for your lot
cause your don't have a map

Although you're
going to the exact same place
God's got you on your own path
where He will allow
you to see and experience His grace

I've read part of the Bible
and I see no reruns yet
so you better get off your seat
and get up and get

Tomorrow's not promised
Can't you tell by my inflection
That the master is coming
and there will be a fruit inspection

When you give you get more
pressed down and given to you
the reason why you're so small
is because of faith underused

But have no fear
the Holy Ghost is a trainer
that will put the flesh in submission
and spiritual ground you will be a gainer

Like Dorothy you had
the power all along
to do what you wanted to do
for God and His kingdom

Reginald O. Johns

OLD GLORY

Don't you feel uncomfortable
Wearing that old sweater
Look child, you ain't poor
I know you can do better

You're walking around here
like you're a beggar or something
Why don't you cash in your inheritance
Start enjoying God's provision

Your lot's not small
King Jesus is your portion
not to forget your reward
This is more than a notion

Sure you had it a long time
and it was beautiful in its day
but it's way too small
for the seams have given away

It's just too small
You've simply outgrown it
that way of doing things
the old way, forget it

Would you use a wood stove
instead of using a bake-o-wave
that kneads and bakes bread
freeing up most of your day

You have to get rid of it
I tell you it's a must
It's beauty has faded
Not too long it will be dust

Have you taken time
to look in your closet
There is a full provision
via a heavenly deposit

Stop wearing the old
Start wearing the new
garments of righteousness
that have been purchased for you

No they're not on credit
the bill's not in the mail
They were purchased by Jesus
when His hands they nailed

to the cross
for just a time as this
when we couldn't cover our sins
with our own righteousness

If you want to know the truth
you look poor indeed
Why don't you look in the mirror
so that you can see
righteousness is by faith
only and indeed
those works don't work
to gain God's favor and mercy

Don't you remember
where we are going tonight
to dine with the King
you must look right

So put on the robe
that God has given you
false modesty isn't becoming
and it certainly doesn't cover you

Reginald O. Johns

Forgiveness without blame
He shares without shame
You're made holy and righteous
by believing in His name

I don't care what the world is wearing
You're not coming with me
It's the truth I'm declaring
Your works don't make you free

Wearing that filthy old rag
you will not make it in
Not to wear what God has provided
is definitely a sin

You make the choice
but take heed to my advice
Cause an invitation to the Marriage Supper
will not happen twice

Scripture Reference - Holy Bible:Matthew 22:8-14 King James Version

GOD'S OFFERING

What more could he give
than His Son
the King of Heaven
the Holy One

A ransom paid
for me He came to save
worth more than the gold
of heaven's pave

He bought life
more abundantly
opened my eyes
for His kingdom to see

Permitted me to enter
through His flesh
nailed and splintered
into a love that cannot
be measured

What more could He give
than His Son
the King of Heaven
the Holy One

He sent His Holy Spirit
to speak His word
so I could hear it
Transforming words upon a page
into a spiritual mirror

For me to see
what I look like
in His sight
Repelling sin's darkness
via a sanctified light

so iniquity would also
not be found in me
because in my heart
I've received the offering
He's given to me

TRADING

When I think
of my quarter and dime
and compare it to
God's Son whose life
was on the line

I ask myself,
"Who taught Him how to trade?"

When I trade with God
it's always in my behalf
sorrow for joy
heaviness for praise
sometimes I must laugh

Don't you ever feel
like you're getting over

on God who sees more
than a roving reporter

yet, He still wants what
I have to give

Perhaps its like those
cheap Mother's Day gifts
you bought when you were a kid

for a mother who would
love you no matter
what you did

or maybe it's like
those pictures you drew in art

Reginald O. Johns

good enough for the trash
yet your mother would not part

with it because
it was made by you

I'm glad we're not
valued in dollars and cents

but by intrinsic worth
Remember the Son He sent

who even said Father
forgive them they know not what they do

Hey God, if a tithe pleases you
I'll give you an offering too!

THE DEAL

If you
take this sorrow
I will praise you

Turn my
mourning into dancing
with my hands
I'll raise you

and

Bless your name

It's a deal
only
if I can
have that sin
and shame and
you'll wear the
robe of righteousness
that bears my name

JESUS

Reginald O. Johns

CONCEPTION

Keep believing
the words
I've given
you

They are
the keys
that unlock
my future
for you

Thoughts that
are good to
fulfill the
expected end

Plans of life
that unfold
from deep
within

Wasn't your
being
created
from a seed

that took time
to develop
once a woman
had conceived

For a God's
that's eternal
9 months
is nothing

Neither is
the time I use
to bring your
vision into
being

Reginald O. Johns

PURPOSE

Reginald O. Johns

BIOGRAPHY

Can we market it
Can we bottle it
Contain it at the seams

So nothing will slip away
The excitement
of a dream

Fulfilled
and complete
By one who has made it

Inspiring others
despite the past to believe
they also can take it

And make something
out of nothing
with our secret ingredients

Faith, hope, and love
cooperation with the Christ I sent

Unlike David
their prayers weren't put to music nor recorded

We'll need writers and producers
so their deeds can be lauded

And acknowledged
and esteemed as a single great event

For even those with silver spoons
must have energy bought and spent

with sweat and perseverance
to create a reality

Reginald O. Johns

of my dream
I placed inside
of them
for all the
world
to
see

INVESTING

deposit yourself
in others and you will never be bankrupt
give and you will receive a
return
of love, comfort, and caring
ears that listen
and hearts that
encourage
when you need a
withdrawal
deposit yourself in others
so that you never
have to
die
without knowing
how to
multiply your
principles

Reginald O. Johns

IF NO ONE EVER DIED

If no one ever died
would we
honor the living just the same

If no one ever died
would we
care about life or think it a game

If no one ever died
would we
consider the maker we would meet

If no one ever died
would we
say thank-you or I love you
or wash one another's feet

Whatever your opinion
death is here to stay

So pour out your goodness
as if it was your very last
day

INVESTMENTS

Love
is planted
in
a
seed

and
grows
into
the
most
beautiful
tree

if
it
is
not
choked
out
by
weeds

and
given
the
attention
it
needs

fertilize
revitalize
your
seed
today

Reginald O. Johns

for
the
harvest
is
worth
more
than
money
can
pay

HELP'S CRY

Emergency
Emergency
Emergency
Break in case of
Emergency

Emergency
Emergency
Emergency
Break in case of
Emergency

Emergency
Emergency
Emergency
Break in case of
Emergency

Fire
Fire
Fire
Burns and devours
a fragile
life

In case of
Emergency
break glass
and
Apply
Love
to Quench
and
Soothe
the
aching
heart

Reginald O. Johns

CAUTION - DO NOT TOUCH

Within a glass
he grew
unable
to be
touched
by hands
that wanted to
mold him
into a caring
man

so
his parents
rodless
used only
what they knew
a voice
raised in
anger
to correct
problems that
grew

his teachers
used a stick
about a yard's
length
to measure
safe distances
to instruct skills to
help him
achieve
one hundred
percent

on tests
that appeared
important
to some

so that
the world
would
become

better doers
but
not
better
be-ers
clothed with humanity

Reginald O. Johns

THE PRESIDENT'S SON

Let the dead bury the dead
and let the living honor their own

They walked and
stood in line
They brought flowers
and took their time

to say
I love you
I cared for you
I will miss you
John Kennedy, Jr.

But
did they call
a relative
that was so far away
How did they remember   .
a living family member
who seems like
they will never
fade away

PULPITS ON PAPER
dedicated to W.E. B. Du Bois

Analyze this man
by the writing
of his hand

Understand what I think
interpret my
symbols of black ink

Letters
and dots
commas
and quotes
explaining my thoughts
emotions
every note

Persuading you
confronting you
to think as I do

If not then
challenging you
to ID the things
motivating you

Off of the paper
into your mind
Understand who I am
'Cause I take the time

to write

Reginald O. Johns

A POEM FOR LORRAINE

Lorraine
the world's changing
just like you said
once 40 now 300 cents
for a loaf of good bread

Lorraine
the world's changing
there's a shifting of wealth
no longer do the Vanderbilts
have to themselves the prestigious top shelf

Lorraine
the world's changing
the nude are accepted on tv
and curse words are
no longer seen as obsenity

Lorraine
the world's changing
our numbers are looking up
instead of 25, now 75% of babies
born are to black mothers without hooking up

Lorraine
the world's changing
choice is a synonym for sin
now all it depends on whose concordance
you're looking in

Lorraine
the world's changing
as a fellow artist what will we say
of the poems, plays, and songs
we created on judgment day

COURAGE

Courage needs
you to open
the can
Give it a five
second shake
and rise again

Courage needs
you to
believe again
that all things
are possible
when you trust
the Lamb

Courage needs
you to speak
the words
of truth

Dispel the
lies sent
to confuse

Courage needs
you to stand
with righteous
indignation

against the
perversion
sent to rape
this nation

of all
that's good, holy
and, Godly

Courage
needs you
more than
Uncle Sam

because only
righteousness
exalts a nation
to be free
and to stand

CONFRONTATION

Face the
dark
as if you are
surrounded by
light

Let not your
heart be troubled
by shadows in
the night

for "Let there be"
creates stars in the
universe

that are intense
enough to enlighten
planets
and support life
on the earth

A CREATOR'S CORRECTION

Green
Blue
Yellow
Black

Magenta
Orange
Red

Hues
and tones

textures
of
brilliance

the world
I created
through
my Son's excellence

Take a lesson
and learn
there is
beauty
in a creation
made with
diversity

if you will
step back
and see

more
than
color

HANDICAPPED...NOT ME!

Why would
I
want to be
color blind

How can
blindness
be a blessing

God created
these eyes
to see

distinguish
and
observe
beauty

Why would
I want to be
color blind

Does a fashion
designer
want to
lose

touch

making
blouses out
of burlap

itchy
and rough

distinguishing
not
between
silk and satin
a wool
polyester
blend

to me
it's just a
sin

Why would I
want to be
color blind

does a conductor
want to be
deaf

throwing
out the window
the importance
of pitch
timbre
a crescendo
or a chord's
emotional
depth

The desire
to make
everyone
the same
is foolish
indeed

for differences
have purpose
and reflect
God's
ingenuity

Skin
darkened
to protect
from sun rays
by melanin

deep brown eyes
able to see in
bright light
equipped
with empowered
vision

Hair that
coils and
turns
allowing the
scalp to
breathe

Different from
the locks
which appear
fine and thin

that collects and
gathers oil
keeping heat in

Everything
has a purpose
far beyond
what we can see

Reginald O. Johns

Cloning
Changing
Mutating
is not the answer
to racial problems
that be

We cannot
pretend that
differences
don't exist

White walling
Black facing
God's creation
due to
ignorance

WISDOM SPEAKS

My son,
you are like a Solomon
that has been raised in a time of peace
not knowing the battles
and the shodding of your feet

My son,
you are like a Solomon
that has been raised in the palace of a king
not knowing the sweat of toil
and the hardship of working

My son,
you are like a Solomon
that has enjoyed the Father's house
his abundant provision
and his bread in your mouth

My son,
you are like a Solomon
who has always been free
not knowing blatant denial
of a racist society

Your eyes have never seen
a white only sign first hand
nor have you had to escape
from slave masters on bare land

so

Don't belittle
your past and foundation
the prayers of your people
who helped build this nation

Reginald O. Johns

Like the Israelites we cried out
to God to make us free
and you are living proof
that God hears sinners like me

so

Don't you forget
that every time we couldn't fight
but sometimes grown men stood
silent with all their might

and

women forgave
for a son's early grave
so that you could walk
upon this marble pave

Our struggle bought your freedom
cause freedom isn't free
someone paid for it by their blood
and even their dignity

Don't forget
and be lazy
because you have a place to rest
made not of straw
but of Macy's finest and best

Just like us
you must sacrifice
Be obedient to God
as you live your life

Cause like Esther and Daniel
you have a place
in the King's palace
Only because of God's grace

OUT OF SIGHT, OUT OF MIND

They build
walls and interstates
around, over
their homes
so we
won't meditate

on the needs
of the poor

or even stop
to contemplate

what I can do
for them

They build
prisons and cart
them away

send down
a television reporter
to give them their say

but if it makes
us uncomfortable
we can click away

the needs
of the poor

They make
standards
to keep them out
build hurdles
higher so
we won't doubt

our need

Reginald O. Johns

for the poor

out of sight
and out of mind
people without worth
or given time
to be seen and heard

the poor of the world

FAMILY

With amazement we discover
their lives were not perfect
under the covers

Regardless of the image
Hollywood projects

Private lives of some
worshipped stars
were actually a wreck

We learn that
marriage times three
really isn't a dream

and being recognized
everywhere you go
isn't all its cracked up to be

Maybe it's not
too bad to be ordinary

working a job
and creating a
loving family

to belong to
and be a part of
is what real life
should be

Us loving one,
Deciding to stick it through

Reginald O. Johns

Breakfast, homework times
and nights at home with the
one God has given to you

Commitment, Fidelity
Transparency, Trust

Must be developed
day by day

In the lives of a man and woman
committed to stay

Until fruit abounds
and can be partaken by many
reproducing more loving relationships
that last longer than their lives will be

FLUFF

It doesn't
matter
if you
choose
pink
or blue

Cotton Candy
is
not
a food
group

Sex
outside
the covenant
of
marriage
will not
fulfill
you

For in
you
is a desire
to belong
to one
whom
you can
be with
until
kingdom
come

Reginald O. Johns

EVE

He looked at Adam
and said
it's not good for man
to be alone

so He
caused him to rest
and removed
a bone beneath his breast

not from his head
nor his feet
nor his thigh
but one bone
of equality
taken
from his side

"This is bone of my
bone and flesh
of my flesh,"
is what Adam had to say

Another
need met
according to God's riches
in glory

Could Adam fathom?
What she would be
A virtuous woman
God had created for he

To compliment him
in areas where he was weak
To help him overcome
and stand on his feet

Woman she was called
for she came from his womb
and was a companion, a wife, and mate
from creation to the tomb

Reginald O. Johns

REVELATIONS

When I opened
my eyes
I saw my
grandfather

Hair of white
bones of strength
wrapped in
loose caramel skin
with an easy grin

When I opened
my eyes
I saw my
grandfather

Full of advice
and wisdom to share

with a listening ear
taking time to care

When I opened
my eyes
I saw my
grandfather

Challenging
and Confronting
Catalyzing a change
in a community and family
where his God reigns

When I opened my eyes
I saw my grandfather

in my Father
sitting across from me

I wonder if one day

Howson McKinley Johns
will ever be seen
in me

Reginald O. Johns

CATCH ME, IF YOU CAN

Ever look back and see
the road you left behind?

Ever stop to wonder
what happened to the time?

Busy, Busy, Busy
Rush, Rush, Rush

Where must I reach
with all the huff and puff?

Can't I sit and dream
and think on things that could be

without someone giving me their
ideas of what the world should be?

How can I ever sit back and absorb
the scenery, if I'm always in a rush?

Doesn't a model have to sit still
to be captured by a brush?

Maybe that's why we have cameras
creating snapshots to remember

A life perpetually in motion
from January to December

EVACUATE - INHABITABLE LANDS MADE BY MAN

The city had no carpet
only hard edges made by man
with lines in it

The city had no curtains
to shade my eyes
from the glare of the sun

only buildings that scraped me
made of glass
Mirrored
Inhibiting my view within

The city had no birds of song
that beckoned me
to sing along

only pigeons that
begged to be fed

The city had no canopy
to give my head a pillow
to rest and dream

only smog
that smothered me

If this is man's Eden
He can have it

and

I'll return to the country
where green is more than

space

Reginald O. Johns

AGREEMENTS

Are the blond dumb
the intelligent nerds
the muscular brutes
That's what I've heard

Are the rich filthy
the spiritual flakes
the athletic dense
I've had all I can take

Gifts are given
not bought or chosen
Nor negotiated by men
who desire to weigh them

Attibute their value
Esteem their worth
making some people better
and others worse

Do you want to be
rich, beautiful, or wise
agree not with those
who inwardly despise

Excellence displayed
to the greatest degree
for you become yoked
with whom you agree

PROGENY

Reginald O. Johns

SPRING'S SURPISE

Pink
Snow

F
     A
        L
            L
               S

in the
warm
wind
outside
my window

blossoms

Reginald O. Johns

KID BREAK

Let's take a break
Just you and me
away from noise
and the old tv

Let's talk, create
draw, and think
with songs of laughter
and crayons pink

A lot of time
we don't need
to enhance the love
in our family

Just give me five
and you will see
how time spent together
strengthens you and me

SNOW

A covering
of white
seems to excite
children of
all ages
when snow
falls the
night
before school
creating a day
full of
cool
fingers
and
hot
cocoa

Reginald O. Johns

NATURE'S WORKOUT

Get ready
Get set
Go!

Storm clouds
race
against the wind

Raindrops
jump
out of the sky

The sun does
pull-ups
over the horizon

while tender leaves
reach
for heaven's high

Petals
push-up
from their stem

Ivy
climbs
over the fence

Blades
of green grass
backbend

to the soil
where
life begins

again
and
again

GOLD

In the midst of green
sunshine
grew

dandilions

short and small

considered by most to be weeds

not esteemed
at all

Its value in
simplicity
no one
ever knew

except for Becky
who received hugs
and
love

when she said,
"Here mommy,
I picked these
for you."

Reginald O. Johns

THINGS THAT MAKE ME HAPPY

I
think
think
think
on things that make me
happy

Songs with La
Tubas with Boomba

Pony tails that curl
on two feet high girls

Band-aids on hands
Rubber on bands

Corn that pops
Spinning colors on tops

Ropes that jump
Bicycle pumps

Monkey with bars
Twinkle in stars

Trucks in dirt
and dust on skirts

Sneakers that run
in green grass in the sun

Lunches in bags
Plastic spiders for gags

Purple candy whistles
Smiles that giggle

Trucks with Ice-cream
that stop when I scream

with treats for ten dimes
Oh, what a time!

Candy on Cotton
How could I have forgotten?

The kisses and love
of my parents and pet slug

Reginald O. Johns

WOW

WOW
Two letters
one word
expressing
extreme excitement

Spurred by
something
seen or heard
motions
seldom
unwisely spent

Retaining its meaning
when read
forwards or rewound

formed by circular lips
sometimes spoken
without a sound

At a stunt
touchdown
or even a stunning diamond

A dark hole
surrounded
by two inverted mountains

Perhaps in every single language
its clearly understood

like the warmth of your heart
when you've done something really good

for another when there is
not an apparent gain

like a comforting rub
for someone who's in pain

or a smile for one
appearing too busy to notice

but is captured by the cheerfulness
of another inviting closeness

Though events worthy of WOWs
may be few and far between

I bet we can squeeze some more
smiles in the mountains
we've been placed between

Reginald O. Johns

PEACE

Reginald O. Johns

THE END

Don't stop living
turn the page
you haven't reached
the end of this age

Don't give up
This is the good part
remember the movies
when you sensed your heart stop

Right before the calvary comes
to save the day
or Lassie saves Timmy
who has drifted away

A change is coming
Be sure, keep living
Turn your page
with much anticipation

Plots well written
don't need a sequel

and based on what
you've been through
your book has no equal

the Author has determined
you finish and complete
your good fight of faith
and the devil you will defeat

With the Word of God
the Holy Spirit has revealed to you
you will rise up and stump
hear his head crunch under your shoe

Reginald O. Johns

EXODUS

When I go
I do not go empty
but with the spoils of my enemy

Jewels of Gold
Jewels of Silver
I shall put on my sons and daughters

I got favor in the
sight of the Egyptians
God brings me out from
under their budens

into a land
He's sworn to me
A land that flows
with milk and honey

REST

He made me
lie down
because I refused
to rest

Coerced me to drink
His living water
as I laid upon
His breast

and just then
it began to
overflow

thanksgiving
gratitude
love
for the Savior
I know

He made me
lie down
on pastures
of green

and caused me to
drink from a still
fulfilling stream

and see beyond
what I can do
for Him

and be strengthened
in the inner man
whom He
is interested in

Reginald O. Johns

THE CALL

I look to Jesus
who bids me to come

walk upon the water
to the sure foundation

The Word of God
tested, tried, and true

Yes, Lord Jesus
I believe you

and will faithfully complete
the task you have
given me to do

THE MATCH

After Jacob wrestled with the angel
I know he had to rest
'Cause when you're wrestling with God
you're wrestling with the best

A God unyielding with power
infinite, holy, divine
Knowing all the tricks of procrastination
that steal His precious time

Never changing His direction,
purpose, nor plan
Waiting for us to surrender
to the control of His hand

Able to stand His ground
unyielding by a bribe
The promises we make
if He would come to our side

Yet, merciful enough that
our spirits He does not crush
Who knows without a doubt
it's His will or bust

Put down your hitch-hiking finger
you can't get away
labor to enter into His rest
Choose to obey

Reginald O. Johns

ABOUT THE AUTHOR

Reginald O. Johns is a graduate of Hampton University and University of Virginia. He is an educator in the public school system and an active member of the Rock Church International Ministries. He currently resides in Hampton, Virginia.

Printed in the United States
954800005B

9 780759 623255